What Happens in Fall?

Leaves in Fall

by Mari Schuh

Bullfrog Books

Ideas for Parents and Teachers

Bullfrog Books let children practice reading informational texts at the earliest reading levels. Repetition, familiar words, and photo labels support early readers.

Before Reading:
- Discuss the cover photo. What does it tell them?

- Look at the picture glossary together. Read and discuss the words.

Read the Book
- "Walk" through the book and look at the photos. Let the child ask questions. Point out the photo labels.

- Read the book to the child, or have him or her read independently.

After Reading
- Prompt the child to think more. Ask: What kinds of trees grow where you live? Do their leaves fall off in the fall? What do you do with the leaves?

Dedicated to Evelyn Quam of Byron, Minnesota.

Bullfrog Books are published by Jump!
5357 Penn Avenue South
Minneapolis, MN 55419
www.jumplibrary.com

Library of Congress Cataloging-in-Publication Data
Schuh, Mari C., 1975-
  Leaves in fall / by Mari Schuh.
    p. cm. — (Bullfrog books. What happens in fall?)
  Summary: "Learn why leaves drop from trees in the fall and learn about different types of leaves. Color photographs and easy-to-read text tell kids all about the changing season"—Provided by publisher.
  Audience: 005.
  Audience: K to grade 3.
  Includes bibliographical references and index.
  ISBN 978-1-62031-059-5 (hardcover : alk. paper) — ISBN 978-1-62496-077-2 (ebook)
  1. Defoliation—Juvenile literature. 2. Leaves—Juvenile literature. 3. Autumn—Juvenile literature. I. Title.
  QK763.S45 2014
  581.4'8—dc23
                                    2013001951

Series Editor: Rebecca Glaser
Series Designer: Ellen Huber
Book Designer: Heather Dreisbach
Photo Researcher: Heather Dreisbach

Photo Credits:
All photos from Shutterstock except: Alamy, 18; Superstock, 5, 15

Printed in the United States of America at Corporate Graphics in North Mankato, Minnesota.
5-2013 / PO 1003
10 9 8 7 6 5 4 3 2 1

Table of Contents

Fall Leaves

Fall is here.

Leaves are falling.
Let's go outside!

5

See the leaves
on the tree?

Leaves make
food for a tree.

They need sunlight
to make food.

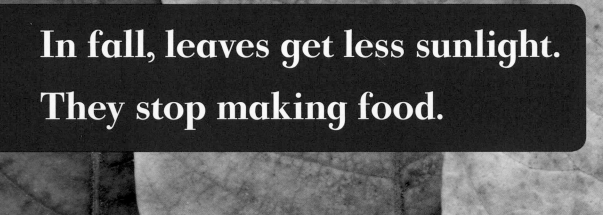

In fall, leaves get less sunlight.
They stop making food.

The leaves change color.

Oak leaves turn red or brown.

Aspen leaves
turn yellow.

The leaf stems
get weak.

The wind blows.

Leaves fall down.

They pile up.

stem

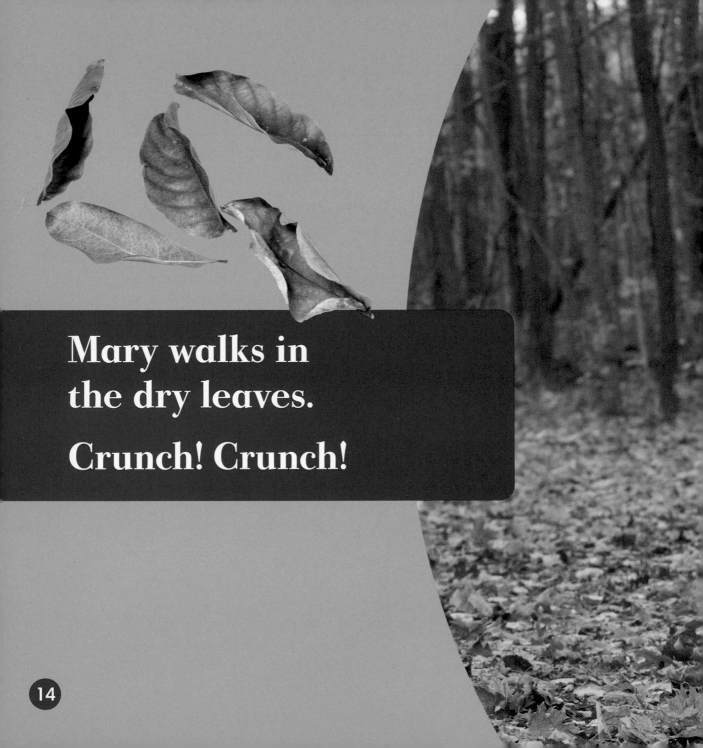

Mary walks in
the dry leaves.

Crunch! Crunch!

Kim rakes the leaves.
She jumps into the pile.

John's mom mows the leaves.
Now the leaves are mulch.
Mulch will help new
plants grow.

mulch

Now the leaves are gone.

The trees are bare.

In spring, leaves will grow again.

Kinds of Leaves

ash leaf

aspen leaf

maple leaf

oak leaf

Picture Glossary

leaf stem
A thin part of a leaf that connects it to a branch.

rake
To gather leaves together in a pile.

mulch
A covering put on soil to make it rich and keep it moist.

sunlight
Light from the sun.

Index

To Learn More

Learning more is as easy as 1, 2, 3.

1) Go to www.factsurfer.com

2) Enter "leavesinfall" into the search box.

3) Click the "Surf" button to see a list of websites.

With factsurfer.com, finding more information is just a click away.